Bad to the Bone
NASTIEST ANIMALS

Red Devil Squid

By John O'Mara

Gareth Stevens
PUBLISHING

Please visit our website, www.garethstevens.com. For a free color catalog of all our high-quality books, call toll free 1-800-542-2595 or fax 1-877-542-2596.

Library of Congress Cataloging-in-Publication Data

O'Mara, John, author.
 Red devil squid / John O'Mara.
    pages cm. — (Bad to the bone. Nasty animals)
 Includes bibliographical references and index.
ISBN 978-1-4824-1966-5 (pbk.)
ISBN 978-1-4824-1965-8 (6 pack)
ISBN 978-1-4824-1967-2 (library binding)
1. Dosidicus—Juvenile literature. 2. Squids—Juvenile literature. I. Title.
QL430.3.O5O43 2015
594.58—dc23

2014031938

First Edition

Published in 2015 by
Gareth Stevens Publishing
111 East 14th Street, Suite 349
New York, NY 10003

Copyright © 2015 Gareth Stevens Publishing

Designer: Michael Flynn and Laura Bowen
Editor: Therese Shea

Photo credits: Cover, pp. 1, 7 (squid), 17 (squid), 21 Carrie Vonderhaar/Ocean Futures Society/National Geographic/Getty Images; cover, pp. 1–24 (series art) foxie/Shutterstock.com; cover, pp. 1–24 (series art) Larysa Ray/Shutterstock.com; cover, pp. 1–24 (series art) LeksusTuss/Shutterstock.com; pp. 5, 9 (both), 13, 15 Franco Banfi/WaterFrame/Getty Images; p. 7 (map) Nelson Marques/Shutterstock.com; p. 11 Mark Conlin/Oxford Scientific/Getty Images; p. 17 (albatross) Fotosearch/Getty Images; p. 19 NOAA/CBNMS/Wikipedia.org.

Printed in the United States of America

CPSIA compliance information: Batch #CW15GS: For further information contact Gareth Stevens, New York, New York at 1-800-542-2595.

Contents

Words in the glossary appear in **bold** type the first time they are used in the text.

Big Squid

A squid has a long, thin, soft body, eight long arms, and two **tentacles**. A red devil squid gets its name because its body can turn red. Red devil squid can be up to 7 feet (2.1 m) long. They may weigh 100 pounds (45 kg). These scary creatures are some of the most **aggressive** squid.

Luckily, red devil squid don't want to eat people. They usually eat creatures less than half their size. However, they destroy their prey, ripping them apart with their incredibly sharp **beak**!

That's Nasty!

Red devil squid have three hearts!

Red devil squid are also called
jumbo squid because of their size.

Where Are They?

Red devil squid are found in the eastern Pacific Ocean. They like to stay in warm waters. They may float near the surface or more than 3,000 feet (914 m) deep, depending on the location of their prey.

It can be hard to track these creatures since they're often so deep. Scientists are using new **technology** to spot them. Red devil squid can be found near Washington, Oregon, and British Columbia, Canada, when waters are warmer there.

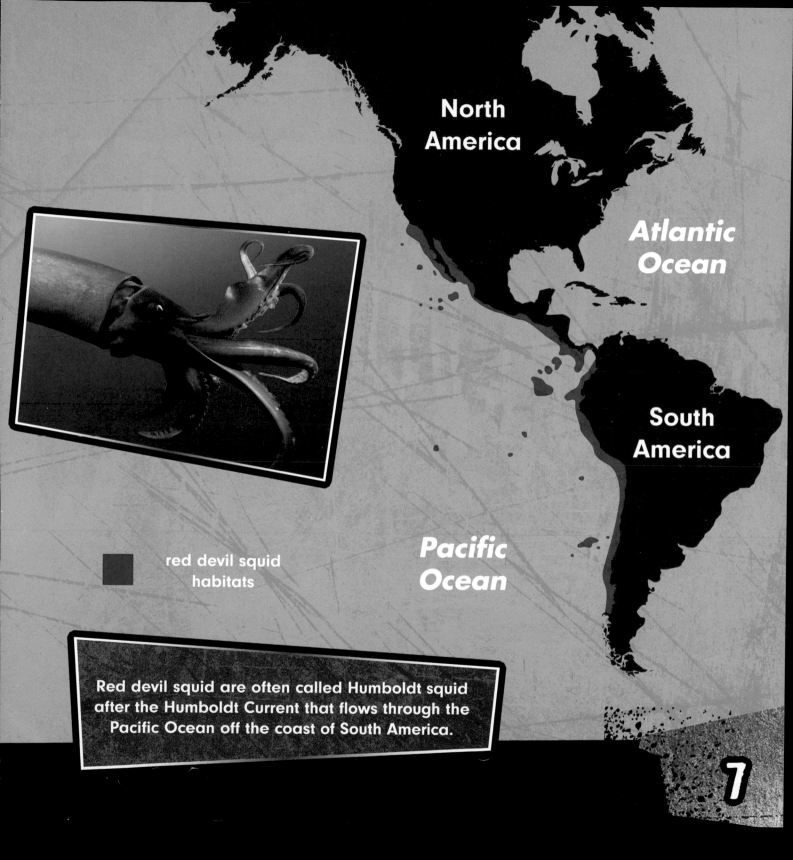

North
America

Atlantic
Ocean

South
America

Pacific
Ocean

red devil squid
habitats

Red devil squid are often called Humboldt squid
after the Humboldt Current that flows through the
Pacific Ocean off the coast of South America.

Amazing Eyes and Arms

Red devil squid have excellent eyesight. A red devil squid's eyes can be as large as 2.5 inches (6.4 cm) across. That's a bit larger than a pool ball! This helps it spot prey even in the dark waters of the deep ocean. Red devil squid prey include fish, **crustaceans**, **mollusks**, and other squid.

Red devil squid have eight arms lined with 100 to 200 suckers each. Once the arms have grabbed hold of something, it's hard for anything to escape. But these aren't the most deadly part of the squid.

That's Nasty!

Each sucker on a red devil squid's arm has up to 36 tiny teeth in it.

teeth in sucker

Any way you look at a red devil squid, it looks strange! It's easy to see the many suckers on its arms in this photo.

A Very Bad Bite

Red devil squid have two long, very quick-moving tentacles that have sharp points called barbs. They use these barbs to stab prey and then bring the prey to their deadly beak, at the base of the arms.

This hard beak is 2 inches (5 cm) long and supersharp. The beak is what the squid uses to kill its prey. It's strong enough to break a fish's backbone so it can't move. Then, the red devil squid rips its prey apart so it's easier to eat.

That's Nasty!

The red devil squid's beak is tougher than metal!

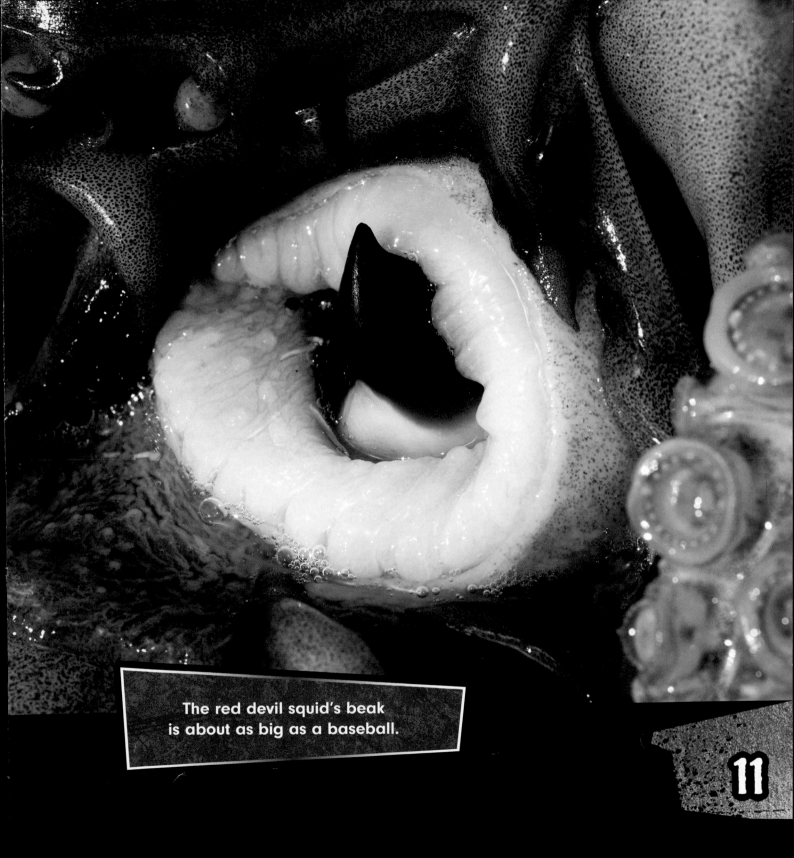

The red devil squid's beak
is about as big as a baseball.

Changing Colors

Squid have a soft body. They have skin that can change colors, including red, purple, and white. Scientists once thought they only changed colors to blend in or hide. Now they think they may do so to **communicate**, though the scientists don't know what the colors mean.

Mexican fishermen gave the red devil squid its name *diablos rojos*, or "red devil," because its skin turns red when it's caught and pulled aboard a boat. The squid keeps fighting, even when it's on a hook.

That's Nasty!

Squid have blue blood!

Red devil squid is used as bait and as food in some parts of the world.

Shoal of Squid

Unlike many other kinds of squid, red devil squid live in groups, called shoals. A shoal may contain up to 1,200 squid. Imagine that many jumbo squid attacking something together! They can move at speeds of up to 15 miles (24 km) per hour.

Divers have reported being attacked by squid! Others say they're just "tasting" with their tentacles to see if people are prey. The squid leave people alone when they find out they're not. Still, this strong squid can be dangerous even if it doesn't mean to be.

That's Nasty!

Red devil squid **squirt** ink to confuse predators. They may squirt ink at fishermen, too!

Squid often attack underwater cameras.
One nearly took off a scientist's mask!
Luckily, the scientist escaped to safety.

Flying Squid!

Red devil squid move by sucking water into their mantle, the main part of the body. Pushing the water out forces the squid to move in the opposite direction. A pair of fins on either side of the red devil squid's mantle help it **steer**. Red devils can move very fast if they're trying to escape predators, such as sharks, whales, tuna, and swordfish.

Red devil squid are part of a group called "flying squid." This group can actually throw themselves out of the water to escape predators!

That's Nasty!

Red devil squid eat their own kind, especially if they find a squid that's hurt or caught in a net.

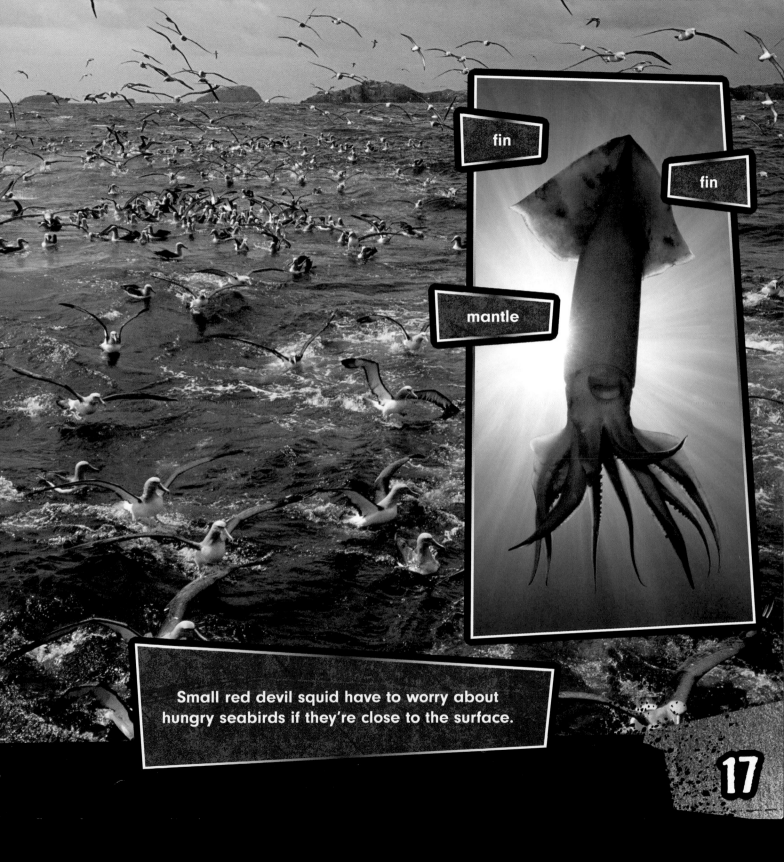

fin

fin

mantle

Small red devil squid have to worry about hungry seabirds if they're close to the surface.

Red devil squid don't live very long, but they grow fast as long as they continue to eat. It's thought that the red devil squid may eat 4 million tons (3.6 million mt) of food a year!

Red devil squid need a lot of **oxygen** for hunting. It's been a mystery to scientists how they spend so much time in deep waters where there's little oxygen. Now scientists know the squid can shut down their body for a time. Then, they can "restart" when they're ready to hunt.

Squid breathe through body parts called gills, like fish do.
By spending time in deep, oxygen-poor waters,
they avoid their predators.

Red Devil Research

Red devil squid have a large brain and are thought to be clever. They usually only live about a year in the wild. They only **mate** once in their life. There's much more to learn about the red devil squid. For example, scientists have never seen their eggs. The squid might hide their eggs at the bottom of the ocean!

Hopefully, in the future, more **research** about this fierce sea creature will let us know about other amazing things they do in the deep sea.

Red Devil Squid: So Nasty!

sharp beak

tentacles with barbs

fast swimmers

arms with toothed suckers

huge eyes with excellent eyesight

Glossary

aggressive: showing a readiness to attack

beak: a part of the mouth that sticks out on some animals and is used to tear food

communicate: to share thoughts or feelings by sound, movement, or other means

crustacean: an animal with a hard shell, jointed limbs, feelers, and no backbone

mate: to come together to make babies

mollusk: an animal that lacks a backbone and has a soft body, such as a snail, clam, squid, or octopus

oxygen: a colorless, odorless gas that many animals, including people, need to breathe

research: studying to find something new

squirt: to force something out of a little opening in a quick stream

steer: to guide something in a direction

technology: the way people do something using tools and the tools that they use

tentacle: a long, thin body part that sticks out from an animal's head or mouth

For More Information

Books

Bergin, Mark. *Sea Creatures*. New York, NY: Windmill Books, 2012.

Owen, Ruth. *Giant Squid and Octopuses*. New York, NY: PowerKids Press, 2014.

Rand, Casey. *Glass Squid and Other Spectacular Squid*. Chicago, IL: Raintree, 2012.

Websites

Humboldt Squid

channel.nationalgeographic.com/channel/ untamed-americas/interactives/humboldt-squid/
Check out this cool interactive activity.

Red Devils

video.nationalgeographic.com/video/humbolt_squid
Watch red devil squid attack a scientist underwater.

Index